Not
Quite
What I Was
Planning

Not Quite What I Was Planning

Six-Word Memoirs
by Writers Famous and Obscure

From SMITH Magazine

Edited by
RACHEL FERSHLEISER
and LARRY SMITH

HARPER  PERENNIAL

NEW YORK • LONDON • TORONTO • SYDNEY • NEW DELHI • AUCKLAND

HARPER ● PERENNIAL

The editors would like to thank SMITH Magazine cofounder Tim Barkow, who was there from word one; Twitter, which helped spread the word fast and far; and the thousands of brilliant memoirists who shared the words in the first place.

Share your six-word story at sixwordmemoir.com or any story at smithmag .net.

All photographs and illustrations are courtesy of the contributors unless otherwise noted.

Photograph on page ii courtesy of Justin Dodd.

HarperCollins books may be purchased for educational, business, or sales promotional use. For information please write: Special Markets Department, HarperCollins Publishers, 10 East 53rd Street, New York, NY 10022.

FIRST EDITION

Designed by Justin Dodd

Library of Congress Cataloging-in-Publication Data is available upon request.

ISBN: 978-0-06-137405-0

08 09 10 11 12 ID/CW 10 9 8 7 6 5 4 3 2

Introduction

LEGEND HAS IT THAT ERNEST HEMINGWAY WAS ONCE challenged to write a story in six words. Papa came back swinging with, **"For sale: baby shoes, never worn."** Some say he called it his best work. Others dismiss the anecdote as a literary folktale. Either way, the six-word story was born, and it's been popping around the writing world for years.

Launched online in 2006, SMITH Magazine celebrates personal storytelling and the ways in which technology has fueled storytelling's growth and infinite possibilities. We like to be both populist and aspirational, blurring the line between professional and amateur. So in November 2006, while thousands of people were cranking out tens of thousands of words during annual National Novel Writing Month, SMITH decided to lower the bar. We gave Hemingway's form a new, personal twist: What would a six-word memoir look like?

We asked our friends; they liked the idea. We ran it by memoirists we admire; they loved the challenge. We shared it with the tech communication wizards at Twitter.com; they wanted to team up to deliver a six-worder a day, free to anyone with a cell phone and a love of stories. With those pieces in place, we invited our readers to submit their short, short life stories for a contest—a battle of brevity.

Soon, six-word wonders were zipping across the Net—from laptops to SMITH, from Twitter to cell phones, from writers to their blogs, from readers to one another. And before we knew it, submissions were coming in by the thousands. Folks from all over the world sent in their sublime frustrations (**"One tooth, one cavity, life's cruel"**) and inspired aspirations (**"Business school? Bah! Pop music? Hurrah!"**), their divine wisdom (**"Savior complex makes for many disappointments"), and deepest inner secrets (**"I like big butts, can't lie"**). And while most of the memoirs were penned by writers who have not been published (until now), others came from household names—from Aimee Mann (whose six is like a short, sweet song) to Mario Batali (who sent a generous half dozen to our table) to Joan Rivers (as outrageous and wonderful as you'd imagine).

We were most struck by the openness of the memoirists—and by their desire to share even more of their lives with perfect strangers. People sent us pictures of the adorable children they'd just admitted, in six words, they regretted having. One woman wrote us a letter detailing the infertility developments that had rendered her hopeful memoir obsolete. "Whole lifetimes happen in people's lives every day," she wrote, "so I suspect many memoirists write what's true at the time only to find their lives drastically different a short distance in the future."

The enthused author of **"Hockey is not just for boys"** sent in a photo essay of chicks with sticks, plus the skate-blade sharpening machine of which she's grown so fond. An artist in San Francisco followed up his book illustration with a comic strip about Anna Nicole Smith. We received photos of deceased wives in bridal gowns, of the tiny headstones of babies lost. An accountant in Florida requested a snail-mail address; soon a packet of miniature origami animals arrived at our office.

Others were rising to the occasion in ways we hadn't expected. We heard that teachers were assigning six-word memoirs to their students; that families were trading six-word memoirs across their dinner tables; that pet fanatics were writing them for their dogs.

We became as obsessed as our own memoirists. Wisdom started to appear everywhere in six-word increments. When a hand dryer in a public restroom bore the graffiti "love me or leave me alone," we took it as a six-word sign from above. We had whole conversations while counting on our fingers (and one thumb) for six-word legitimacy. We found ourselves debating the validity of hyphens over dinner and drinks. (Just how many words is "three-legged cat"?)

The fruit of this amazing response? You're holding it in your hands.

One of the delights of reading six-word memoirs is imagining the writer behind those few carefully chosen words. Despite the well-documented dangers of assumption, we were surprised to learn how many of the real-life writers were nothing like we expected.

The bittersweet **"Cursed with cancer. Blessed with friends"** came not from a wise, optimistic grandmother, but a nine-year-old thyroid-cancer survivor. The brave girl's mother wrote to say that her daughter had sat alone at the computer for hours selecting her words, and then checked SMITH each day, hoping to see her name on the screen. The poignant **"I still make coffee for two"** didn't come from the shaky hand of an elderly widower, but a recently dumped twenty-seven-year-old dude with a fondness for caffeine. After months of reading six-word memoirs barely noticing the writer's name, sometimes we were delighted by words seven and eight. After all, could you ask for a better life story from Deepak Chopra's son than **"Soul'd out so I could prophet"**?

This book is a glorious mishmash of these and myriad other voices; it's a thousand little windows into humanity—six words at a time. Whether the results are shocking, strange, silly, or sad, we hope you'll agree that they are always entertaining, often inspiring, and totally addictive.

In the autobiographical spirit of SMITH Magazine, the photos and illustrations that appear here arrived from the writers themselves. To see hundreds of images we didn't have room for, plus new memoirs every day, go to **www.sixwordmemoir.com**. While you're there, you just might be struck by an overwhelming desire to supply a six-word memoir of your own. And why wouldn't you: Everyone has a story—what's yours?

The editors of SMITH Magazine
September 2007
New York, NY

Not
Quite
What I Was
Planning

After Harvard, had
baby with crackhead.

—*Robin Templeton*

Seventy years, few tears, hairy ears.

—*Bill Querengesser*

Watching quietly from
every door frame.

—*Nicole Resseguie*

Catholic school backfired.
Sin is in!

—*Nikki Beland*

Savior complex makes for
many disappointments.

—*Alanna Schubach*

Nobody cared, then they did.
Why?

—*Chuck Klosterman*

Some cross-eyed kid,
forgotten then found.

—*Diana Welch*

She said she was negative.
Damn.

—*Ryan McRae*

Born in the desert,
still thirsty.

—*Georgene Nunn*

A sake mom, not soccer mom.

—*Shawna Hausman*

I asked.

They answered.

I wrote.

—*Sebastian Junger*

No future, no past. Not lost.

—*Matt Brensilver*

Extremely responsible, secretly longed for spontaneity.

—*Sabra Jennings*

```
Joined Army. Came out.
Got booted.
```

—*Johan Baumeister*

Almost a victim of my family.

—*Chuck Sangster*

The psychic said I'd be richer.

—*Elizabeth Bernstein*

Grumpy old soundman
needs love, too.

—Lennie Rosengard

Mom died, Dad screwed us over.

—Lesley Kysely

Painful nerd kid,
happy nerd adult.

—Linda Williamson

Write about sex,
learn about love.

—Martha Garvey

Stole wife. Lost friends.
Now happy.

—Po Bronson

Fourteen years old,
story still untold.

—David Gidwani

One long train ride to darkness.

—Wayne Colodny

Wolf! She cried.
No one listened.

—May Lee

I'm my mother and I'm fine.

—K. Bertrand

All day I dream about sex.

—Guro Tupchileshtoff

I still make coffee for two.

—*Zak Nelson*

I like girls. Girls like boys.

—Andrea Dela Cruz

Never should have bought that ring.

—Paul Bellows

Sold belongings. Became Itinerant Poetry Librarian.

—Sara Wingate Gray

Tombstone won't say "had health insurance."

—Dean Haspiel

Stranded by ten-thousand-mile crush.

—Will Cockrell

Wasted time regretted
so life reinvented.

−Vicky Oppus

College was fun.
Damn student loans.

−Randy Boland

`Semicolons;`
`I use them to excess.`

−Iris Page

God chose. Said no. Now what?

−Adam Blackman

Time heals all wounds? Not quite.

−Jonathan Miles

Oldest of five. Four degrees. Broke.

—*Kaitlin Walsh*

Made a mess. Cleaned it up.

—*Amy Anderson*

A crush on Susan Sarandon.
Unrequited.

—*Willy Edge*

Says deaf boyfriend:
   you're too quiet.

—*Anna Jane Grossman*

Alive 38 years, feels like 83.

—*Bryan Lowry*

My family is overflowing with therapists.

—Shaina Feinberg

Boy, if I had a hammer.

—Tim Barkow

We still don't hear a single.

—Adam Schlesinger

Canada freezing. Gotham
beckons. Hello, Si!

—Graydon Carter

Years in the closet.
Why? Why?

—Michael Callahan

Docens liberos veritatem
vitam mihi docet.

—Michael Farmer

I did ask to live backwards.

—Helen Glynn

Forest peace, sharing vision,
always optimistic.

—Dr. Jane Goodall

Bespectacled, besneakered,
read and ran around.

—Rachel Fershleiser

Supported the sublime
with uncurbed
enthusiasm.

—Jeff Newelt

Followed white rabbit.
Became black sheep.

—Gabrielle Maconi

Middle of seven
made me me.

—Susan Sinnott

The woman formerly
known as Marissa.

—Mimi Ghez

Followed yellow brick road.
Disappointment ensued.

—Kelsey Ochs

Nerdy girl smutmonger.
Now, baby fever.

—Rachel Kramer Bussel

Born free, but lost my country.

—*Ted O'Brien*

Recent doctorate means overeducated
and underemployed.

—*Philip Sternberg*

Taking a lifetime to grow up.

—*Mirona Iliescu*

Living for Jesus because
earth sucks.

—*Johnny Johnson*

Bad brakes discovered at high speed.

—*Paul Schultz*

Danced in
Fields
of Infinite
Possibilities.

—*Deepak Chopra*

Soul'd out so I could
prophet.

—*Gotham Chopra*

Strange name.
Transparent shame.
    Instant fame.

—Bumble Ward

In the office. It smells here.

—Meera Parthasarathy

I am trying, in every regard.

—Lionel Shriver

Birth, childhood,
    adolescence, adolescence,
      adolescence, adolescence . . .

—Jim Gladstone

**Happiest when ignoring
huge financial debt.**

—Ayanna Bryan

—Keith Knight

Not pretty enough
  so now unemployed.

—*Stacey Smith*

I threw away my teddy
bear.

—*Margot Loren*

Mistakes were made,
but smarter now.

—*Christine Triano*

**Likes everything too
much to choose.**

—*Rachel Lindenthal*

Curly haired sad kid chose fun.

—*Stacy Abramson*

Now I blog and drink wine.

−Peter Bartlett

Egomaniac with inferiority
complex defies odds.

−Lynne Vittorio

I thought I was someone else.

−Tysa Goodrich

Dancing for now,
one day farming.

−Eleanor Carpenter

Amazing grace: born naked,
clothed others.

−Mark Budman

Followed rules, not dreams. Never again.

—Margaret Hellerstein

My baby's name was Sydney Jane.

—Margot Bertoni

Love the men.
Hate the commitment.

—Lindsay Filz

I grew and grew and grew.

—Randy Newcomer

Starving artist.
Lucky break.
Life downhill.

—Will Samson

Changing mind postponed
demise by decades.

—Scott O'Neil

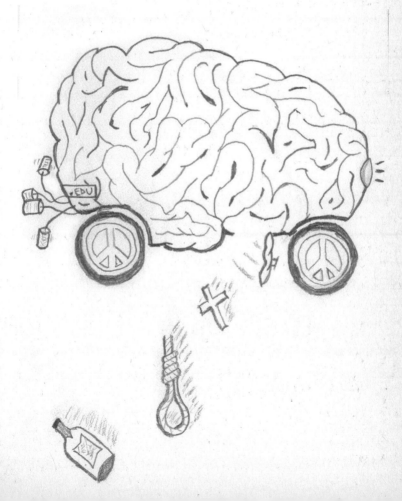

My spiritual path is 100 proof.

—John House

Wanted world,
   got world plus lupus.

—Liz Futrell

Yes to every date, met mate.

—Maria Dahvana Headley

The Hustle: turn champion
into sucker.

—Amarillo Slim

I was born
some assembly
required.

—Eric Jordan

I drank too much last night.

—*Meg McIntyre*

Study mathematics. Marry slut.
Sum bad.

—*Dan Robinson*

Took scenic route, got in late.

—*Will Blythe*

Raised Jehovah's Witness.
Excommunicated at 22.

—*Kyria Abrahams*

**I like big butts,
can't lie.**

—*Dave Russ*

I'm enjoying

downward

even this

dance.

—*Colum McCann*

Without ideas, intelligence could not exist!

—Ornette Coleman

I hope to outlive my regrets.

—Bob Logan

All night phone calls
complete me.

—Harry Manning

Tragic childhood can
lead to wisdom.

—Kristin Ahlemeier-Olfe

Sweet wife, good sons—
I'm rich.

—Roger Waggener

Barrister, barista,
what's the diff, Mom?

—Abigail Moorhouse

Mom, Dad. Daphne, Owen.
Who's next?

—Sean Wilsey

Which comes first:
tequila or accident?

—Penelope Whitney

`Doing more for less is life.`

—Rondell Conway

Cried. Defied, Denied. Sighed.
Died. Reapplied.

—Josh Gosfield

A sundress will solve
life's woes.

—Kristen Grimm

I recognize red flags
faster, now.

—Barbara Burri

I sucked even the lobster legs.

—Rufus Griscom

Anything's possible with
an extension cord.

—billySIRR

In and out of hot water.

—Piper Kerman

Life has gone to the dogs.

—Ted Rheingold

Moved to SF. Geek, not gay.

—*Ryan King*

Nothing profound,
I just sat around.

—*Daniel Rosenburg*

Found true love,
married someone
else.

—*Bjorn Stromberg*

Others left early: he
continued looking.

—*Anthony Swofford*

Shy Jersey kid,

overcompensating ever since.

—*Ariel Kaminer*

Dad died, mom crazy, me, too.

—*Moby*

Being a
monk stunk.
Better gay.

—*Bob Redman*

Quiet guy; please pay closer attention.

—*Jonathan Lesser*

Oklahoma girl meets world.
Regrets it.

—*Gretchen Wahl*

Life was but a dream,
merrily.

—*Paul W. Morris*

Happiness is a warm salami sandwich.

—*Stanley Bing*

Creative and destructive
in many ways.

—Meghan DeRoma

I sell hamburgers,
and french fries.

—Richard Maurer

Coffee junkie journalist
seeks trendy nerd.

—Jackie Olson

Fight. like. hell.
for. the. living.

—Susie Bright

On her birthday, my life
began.

—Lisa Parrack

Xenophile escapist tumbleweed globetrots, finds self.

—*Dominic Arizona Bonuccelli*

The shit invariably
hits the fan.

—Ashleea Nielsen

Blogging is easy.
Writing is hard.

—Jennifer Shreve

Quit Uni, have baby, now bored.

—Samantha Ng

I fell in love with Charlie.

—Kristine Allouchery

And he nerded
as never before.

—Jon Thysell

Iowa to Brooklyn,
     hair growing everywhere.

—William Johnson

Fix a toilet, get paid crap.

—Jennifer James

Tow truck drivers
are my psychiatrists.

—Joanne McNeil

Should have used
condom that time.

—Rob Bigelow

**Macular degeneration.
Didn't see that coming.**

—Ian Gould

Fifty years so far.
Happened fast.

—Mark Michaelson

Atheist plus Methodist make
Jewish children.

—Richard Michelson

Infinite calm beset with emotional
architecture.

—DJ Spooky

Won the fight;
lost the girl.

—Jim O'Grady

Near death experiences
are my forte.

—Anna Mauser-Martinez

Illustration by Josh Neufeld

Fight, work, persevere—
gain slight notoriety.

—*Harvey Pekar*

**Lived in moment
until moment sucked.**

—Janine Goss

She said nothing could go
wrong.

—Derek Powazek

Laughing until I pee my pants.

—Carolyn Waller

`Go find your father; my life.`

—Adam Danielson

Life goal:
Maximum results, minimal effort.

—Phil Kahn

Clawed my way out of Tennessee.

—Nae Shell

Quite undecided, yet hopefully
unsatisfied, generally.

—Daniel Gumbiner

Took a spectacle, made
it sport.

—Dana White

`Slightly psychotic,`
`in a good way.`

—Patricia Neelty

She walked barefoot
in wet cement.

—Michelle Pinchev

As a child, nomadic. Now static.

—Kristin Gotski

Mushrooms.
Clowns.
Wands.
Five.
Wig.
Thatched.

—Amy Sedaris

Found true love after
nine months.

—Jody Smith

Hillbilly does right
by his teeth.

—Jason Snyder

No words can describe my life.

—John Baldridge

Afraid of everything.
Did it anyway.

—Ayse Erginer

On the playground, alone.
1970, today.

—Charles Warren

I wrote it all down somewhere.

—*Ben Greenman*

Inside suburban mom
    beats urban heart.

—*Julie Goss*

Missed Halley's Comet.
Miss virginity too.

—*Yoz Grahame*

Not a good Christian,
but trying.

—*Alexander Tsai*

Red diaper baby, hippie,
bourgeoise adult.

—*Adrienne Ross*

Lost and found, rescued by dog.

—*Gail Reilly*

Afraid of becoming like my mother.

—*Jocelyn Pearce*

Goodbye Fat Kim: I now live.

—*Kim Kaufman*

Two boys, my life,
conquering autism.

—*Michelle DePasquale*

Montana Jew—drives Toyota;
holsters pen.

—*Michael Finkel*

Mistakenly kills kitten. Fears anything delicate. —Susan Henderson

Illustration by Brian P. McEntree

What the hell.
Might as well.

—Nancy London

Hexed:
curse of the happy childhood.

—Cree McCree

Sometimes I'm crazy,
sometimes I'm sane.

—Bella Von Phul

Can't tonight,
watching *Law & Order.*

—Rory Evans

Musician gone bad.
Darn law school!

—Stephen Adams

I take photographs. I see life.

—Daniel James

Hippie parents.
Early independence.
Surprising success.

—Darci Groves

My life's a bunch of almosts.

—Shari Bonnin

Struggled with how
the mind works.

—Steven Pinker

It's not you. It's me. Honest.

—Allison Glock

Brought it to a boil, often.

–Mario Batali

Scribbling twit dreaming
lit every minute.

—Jamie Grove

Thought I would have
more impact.

—Kevin Clark

This is aggression in
pink, Mom.

—Nicole Tourtelot

```
Graduated May.
21 June.
Married July.
```

—Amara Rockar

Oh, to have just one puff!

—Suhana Selamat

Bad reputation,
such a good girl.

—Erin Oldroyd

Mom left. Returned! Left.
Reconciliation! Cancer.

—Kelly Streit

Laughing intellectual
ronin danced,
unlearning lies.

—Tom Buckner

At the end of normal street.

—Tracey Morgan

Found great happiness in
insignificant details.

—Alisdair McDiarmid

Spent life looking
for dead people.

—*Melody Lassalle*

Forty Five.

Never Married.

Oh poo.

—*Sonia Oney*

Enjoying my fuck ups too much.

—*Susan Crippin*

My reach always
exceeds my grasp.

—*Ray Garraud*

Marked time till 55,
reborn thereafter.

—*Doug Fraser*

Details.
I really hate
    drawing backgrounds.

—Starline Hodge

Four children in four decades; whew!

—*Loretta Serrano*

An unusual turn of gender circumstances.

—*Dragana Varadinac*

Hiding in apartment knitting against depression.

—*Laurie White*

She kissed me and said yes!

—*Ricardo Saramago*

Dabbler in much, expert in none.

—*Joan Cady*

Once wed,
      twice loved,
            past prime.

—Betty Black

Grading AP essays,
I crave Tolstoy.

—Carinna Tarvin

Always dreamt of kissing pretty girls.

—Jessica Furey

I lost god. I found myself.

—Joe Kimmel

Everyone who loved me is dead.

—Ellen Fanning

Life is circular. Caring for parents. Life is

—*Timothy McGrath*

**It was embarrassing,
so don't ask.**

—Alex Lindquist

Verbal hemophilia.
Why can't I clot?

—Scott Mebus

Time to start over again,
again.

—Dan Petronelli

```
Always even keel
except when sailing.
```

—Maryann Pirrotta

Still lost on road less traveled.

—Joe Quesada

Over fifty, still a Boy Scout!

—Jerry Richstein

The car accident
changed my life.

—Kristin Stanefski

Said goodbye,
hasn't shut up since.

—Michael Collins

Burned my bridges and
my britches.

—Dave Zablocki

Trains, planes, thumb;
then children come.

—Karen Franklin

Older now, I draw myself better.

—*Peter Arkle*

Batteries are cheap.
Who needs men?

—Rebecca McLenna

Clueless meets Ophelia,
without the suicide.

—Larisa Ballinger

Atheist alcoholic gets
sober through God.

—Bob Todd

Discovered moral code
via Judy Blume.

—Beth Greivel

Artsy married Fartsy,
has two kids.

—Mary Organ

Anything possible—but I was tired.

—Cheryl Family

I ate, drank, and was hairy.

—Yianni Varonis

Girlfriend is pregnant, my husband said.

—Shonna MacDonald

I am awfully bored at work.

—Chris Ponchak

Learned reading, writing,
forgot arithmetic.

—Elizabeth Gruner

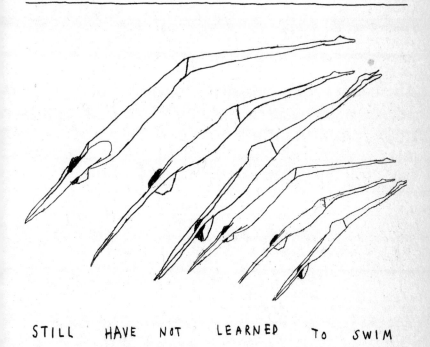

STILL HAVE NOT LEARNED TO SWIM

—Lauren Redniss

Trying to medicate my redneck past.

—*Garrett Sparks*

Lucky in love,
unlucky in metabolism.

—*Leah Weathersby*

I live the perfect
imperfect life.

—*Paul Lore*

Ate caterpillars.
Still won't grow up.

—*Chris Jackson*

Wannabe heroine but
just Plain Jane.

—*Tanya Holland*

Civil servant answers phone after five.

—*Jason Prince*

Glass half full;
pockets half empty.

—*Marina Guthrie*

We undercover agents
need mental toughness.

—*Joe Pistone*

Rebel librarian on sabbatical from boys.

—*Heather Meagher*

Arthur-ectomy taking years!
Beware: wed cautiously.

—*Natalie Windsor*

Woman Seeks Men—
High Pain Threshold.

—Yin Shih

No Wife.
No Kids.
No Problems.

—Rip Riley

You are all in my imagination.

—Becky Weinberg

School geek married a
luscious cheerleader.

—Christopher Clukey

I couldn't protect me
from myself.

—Patrick Eleey

Eat mutate aura
amateur auteur true.

—*Jonathan Lethem*

Aspiring lady pirate, disillusioned, sells boat.

—*Diana White*

Kentucky trash heap yields unexpected flower.

—*John Kurtz*

Married for money.
Divorced for love.

—*Rosie Abraham*

My life is a beautiful accident.

—*J. D. Tenuta*

Thank God I lived through Vietnam.

—*Captain John Irving*

Meat and potatoes man
goes vegetarian.

—Perette Lawrence

Smart, tall, independent woman.
Men scarce.

—Annie Schmidt

I was and now I'm not.

—Gayla Buyukas

Oh sweet nectar of life, coffee.

—Daniel Axenty

Young, skinny, ridiculed.

Old, skinny, envied.

—Phil Sweet

No shit I'm critical—
you're flawed.

—Elizabeth Koch

It's pretty high. You go first.

—Alan Eagle

One tooth,
one cavity,
life's cruel.

—John Bettencourt

In a Manolo world, I'm Keds.

—Colleen Cook

Lonely gay
hates work,
loves play.

—Ray Ivey

Wasn't noticed so
I painted trains.

—Mare 139

Chinese immigrant loathing drama
in Anaheim.

—Eric Wong

Running away:
best decision I made.

—Stephen Elliott

I served my debt to society.

—Michael Frisch

Scarred by 9/11;
helped by penguins.

—Audrey Blackburn

Fleeting nights, cloudy mornings,
coffee's ablution

—Heath Hardin

When she proposed, I said yes.

—Josh Neufeld

Black Latina. Slave ship stopped
everywhere.

—Veronica Chambers

My heart is deaf,
head dumb.

—David Matthews

My first concert: Zappa. Explains everything.

—Janet Tashjian

Nobody knows how
I have suffered.

—Tim Hall

Dweeb, pussy . . . stronger than
anyone knows.

—Jim S.

**Wandering imagination
opens doors to paradise.**

—Rebecca Perlstein

**After eighteen years,
sold my book.**

—Susan Runholt

Too many lovers—
too little time.

—Joel Kincaid

Confused Communist child,
enlightened American engineer.

—Attila Kalamar

Couldn't cope so I wrote songs.

—Aimee Mann

Timid teacher takes
'tude from tykes.

—Kathy Gates

Angry guy gets law
license, sues.

—Bryan Gates

Long lost girl
recently found, unharmed.

—Tracy Bishop

Gave commencement address,
became sex columnist.

—Amy Sohn

3,000 miles away from
the truth.

—Michael Slenske

Mormon economist marries
feminist. Worlds collide.

—*Michael McBride*

Mormon feminist loves
husband, hates patriarchy.

—*Caroline Kline*

Followed dim shapes through narcotic haze.

—John Law

Mom, Dad have dementia.
Got gun?

—Carol Belding

Born a twin, died a loner.

—Heather Thompson

```
Young optimist:
proven wrong.
Prematurely old.
```

—Buzzy Porter

It was worth it, I think.

—Annette Laitinen

Students laughed appreciatively. The
professor relaxed.

—*Laurie Hensley*

Drink because I am a poet.

—*Maria Essig*

People always pronounce
my name incorrectly.

—*Linnea Jimison*

**Dorothy Gale had the
right idea.**

—*Pamela Vissing*

Dropped out, got
out, lucked out.

—*Ben Kweller*

Take a left turn, then fly.

—Hillary Carlip

I was never the pretty one.

—*Joan Nesbit Mabe*

Born at 23,
childhood doesn't count.

—*Krissy Karol*

Perpetual work in
progress,
need editor.

—*Sherry Fuqua-Gilson*

Left Aruba for
Maryland.
Pretty dumb.

—*Barbara Phillips-Seitz*

I was the only planned
sibling.

—*Mary Sebas*

Age grows,
I've finally accepted me.

—Kate Mammolito

Paralyzed at fifty,
life still nifty.

—Gib Henderson

Snuggling, setups.
These are my specialties.

—Laura Cooper

Was big boy, now
little man.

—Chris Cooper

Lost Colorado wife.
Found Seattle life.

—Jason Cain

Ex-con making good
on lifestyle promise.

—Doug Houston

Canoe guide, only got lost once.

—Taylor Stump

**Aging late bloomer
yearns for do-over.**

—Sydney Zvara

American backbone,
Arab marrow,
much trouble.

—Rabih Alameddine

Memory was my drug of
choice.

—Pea Hicks

Liars, hysterectomy *didn't* improve sex life!

—*Joan Rivers*

Mom, sorry I moved to U.S.

—*Yuri Fukazawa*

Unhappy joke writer
hugs her chihuahua.

—*Jessica Salmonson*

Boys liked her.
She preferred
books.

—*Anneliese Cuttle*

Wife died young; on the mend.

—*Sumit Paul-Choudhury*

I'm ten, and have
an additude.

—*Tillie Seger*

**Gay physician designed
life-saving AIDS drugs.**

—Laurent Fischer

Never lived up to my potential.

—Leslie Sterling

Girl from Wisconsin
got to leave.

—Catherine Michalec

Tequila. Amnesia. Coincidence?
I think not.

—Larry Caraviello

Carbohydrates call my
name every day.

—Mary Petersdorf

Never really finished
anything, except cake.

—*Carletta Perkins*

Cursed with cancer.
Blessed with friends.

–Hannah Davies

```
Crappy parents
killed
my self esteem.
```

–Julie Doherty

Lonely artist turned
waitress in love.

–Gretchen Bone

Does my biological mother
cry sometimes?

–Steven Schmidt

My life is just like yours.

–Matt Stephens

Some collect coins,
I collect diplomas.

—Srini Rajagopalan

Bipolar at 12, lithium at 36.

—Linda Hatfield-Southern

Navy dependent writes
American haiku poetry.

—Craig Jones

If Eliza Doolittle
wore cowboy boots . . .

—Dixie Friedman

Ex-wife and contractor
now have house.

—Drew Peck

Fifteen years since last professional haircut.

—Dave Eggers

Midlife crisis uncovers queer intellectual's talent.

—Donald W. Jacobson

Fat jolly bearded origami-folding accountant.

—Gary Mullings

Lucky in everything
else but love.

—Eliot Sheridan

Mixed blood.
I am America's future.

—Holly Santiago

I'm just here for the beer.

—Alex Vournas

With three cats
I'm never unloved.

—Cynthia Macdonald

Missing limb,
cruel world,
love overcomes.

—James Mallon

Divorced twice,
lived happily ever after.

—Susan Guyaux

Torrential tryst.
Terrible twins.
Tied tubes.

—M. Brenner

Can my words have
footnotes, please?

—Amy Harbottle

So it goes,
a tad askew.

—*Michael Dickter*

Alas, a farewell to legs. Next!

—*Allen Rucker*

Came, saw, conquered,
had second thoughts.

—*Harold Ramis*

Left a desert for a
wasteland.

—*James Slone*

**City streets,
saggy shoes,
and poetry**.

—*Arianna Kandell*

The weather is better up
here.

—*Brad Wieners*

Beat death thrice.
Still not religious.

—Shan Palmer

Found love.
Got hitched in Vegas.

—Jami Brandli

Baby dyke now raising
two babies.

—Andrea Selch

Stoned. Boned.
Where am I now?

—Sherry Levy

New Jersey to California.
Thank God.

—Ayelet Waldman

Town car,
   tailored suit,
      dirty nails.

—Nicole Blades

**Bipolar secretary
girlfriend mama hen
oddball.**

—Teressa Fly

Learning to be great
at mediocrity.

—Christopher Reiger

**Jewfro and glasses,
laughter and yoga.**

—Deborah Greene

I fell far from the tree.

—Rebecca Stadolnik

The image was large with silence.

—*Elizabeth Raab*

Chinese? American?
Chinese-American?
    The confusion endures.

—*Paul Chin*

After your jump,

the net appears.

—*Vincent Lauria*

Talkative female Trekkie
married male gamer.

—*Sarah Hairston*

I colored outside of the lines.

—*Jacob Thomas*

Without me, it is
just aweso.

—*Chris Madigan*

```
Me: consistently avoiding
   death since 1978!
```
                    —Daniel Fowlkes

I think, therefore I am bald.

                    —Dickie Widjaja

Should not have eaten
those mushrooms.

                    —Emilie Raguso

Wanked furiously.
Married. Furious no more.

                    —John Heppolette

Wealthy woman
escapes
with handsome
mailman.

                    —April Shewan

IBM brat broke back;
twins, Mac.

—*John Hockenberry*

Love annihilated a
thirty-year age difference.

—*Betsy Smith*

Saw, interpreted, mourned,
hoped, then preached.

—*Douglas Rushkoff*

Even the quietest

sounds

make noise.

—*Paul Boggan*

I grew up in a cemetery.

—*Rachael Hanel*

Many hands have kept me afloat.

—*Nick Flynn*

Man of the world = alien immigrant.

—Rajat Suri

Ran away with
circus; never
returned.

—Ellia Bisker

I managed not to
destroy anything.

—Tucker Frazier

All of my students hate me.

—Sharon Fishfeld

Gay white African
emigrates, finds love.

—Graham Coppin

ABCs

MTV

SATs

THC

IRA

NPR.

—Jancee Dunn

Buxom songstress loves love
and chocolate.

—Angie Arnold

Blade cuts,
blood runs,
scars remain.

—Heather Hudgins

Did I miss a deadline again?

—Bruce McGill

Walking the green mile:
finally free.

—Alejandro Echeverra

Redhead woman,
raucous curves,
makes music.

—Shannon Russell

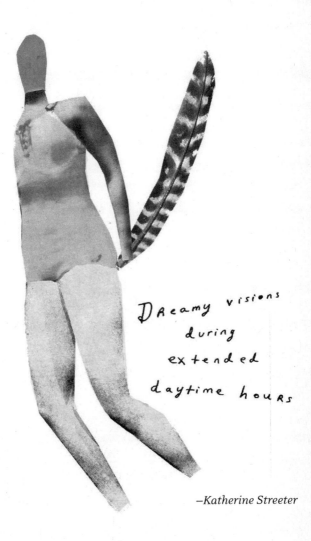

DReamy visions
during
extended
daytime hours

—Katherine Streeter

Love drama,
    just not my own.

–Sam Zalutsky

I wouldn't change it a bit.

–Ann Paxton

Saw the
world; now
where's home?

–Hannah Silverstein

Nose broken, beauty queen
changes profession.

–Dan Rubin

Nineteen forty-nine to two
thousand . . . something.

–Anne Greer

Blinked! Winked!
I am halfway through!

—Vinod Pillai

Arms: full. Life: not so much.

—Renee James

Quietly
cultivating my
inner Lynda Carter.

—Joanna Sheehan

Many risky mistakes,
very few regrets.

—Richard Schnedl

Six kids; life stranger than fiction!

—Deborah Carson

He left me for good eventually.

—Audrie Lawrence

Liberal at 18.
Conservative by 40.

—Pat Ryan

Would you like fries
with that?

—Scott Northrup

I won Miss Union
Pier 1952.

—Elaine Yonover

Legs spread,
I withheld my
intelligence.

—Christine Granados

Next time—

better parents, better hair.

—Ruth Romano

Little bit Lucy,
tempered by Ethel.

—Tami Maus

Traversing Earth together,
chasing elusive answers.

—Paul Barber

**Considered life, then death.
Step, repeat.**

—Paul Pope

Hockey is not just for boys.

—Alexandra Duplin

Artist, disabled.
Feeling mislabeled.
Ambitions tabled.

—*Patrick Dentinger*

Fell in love. Married.
Divorced. Repeat.

—Lori McLeese

Never liked the taste
of beets.

—Michael Pemberton

```
Underachieving
pleasure punk seeks
constant gratification.
```

—Dennis Elj

Always working on
the next chapter.

—Milan Pham

**Business school? Bah!
Pop music? Hurrah!**

—Max Robins

Happy now that I know myself.

—*Anne Maiwald*

Polka-dotted mayhem
and decadent disasters.

—*Candace Locklear*

Beach mama blissfully buoys
burgeoning brood.

—*Elizabeth Barr*

Risked it all;
wasn't quite enough.

—*Greta Orris*

I write because I can't
sleep.

—*Ben Mezrich*

Sperm too potent,
now have triplets.

−Renee Schunk

Never fear.
  Truffle season is near.

−Barry Glassner

```
Yes, you can edit
this biography.
```
−Jimmy Wales

**The best hair, the worst
shpilkes.**

−Joanna Arkans

Katie180, you make
my heart crazy.

−John Patrick Zito

Started

small,

grew,

peaked,

shrunk,

vanished.

—George Saunders

**My daughter's baby,
   inconvenient and incredible.**

−Laurie White

Mom blames musical theater.
I disagree.

−Dan Sigale

Insubordinate alien bookworm found
America, freedom.

−Katherine Scourtes

Big, little sister,
stuck in middle.

−Joanna Lilly

Short kid moves West;

climbs mountains.

−Mark Lilly

Multiple miscarriages.
Cousin will carry baby.

—Joanna Brody

Alone at home, cat on lap.

—Christopher Goldthwaite

Poet locked
in body
of contractor.

—Marilyn Hencken

And I never did sober up.

—Ray Overfield

Three marriages.
Thirteen novels.
Sleep's overrated.

—Jane Heller

World backpacking decade
ends with minivan.

–Cindi Hounton

Educated too much,
lived too little.

–Dan Vance

Lapsed Catholic;
failed poet;
unpublished prayers.

–Marc Sheehan

Twin girls,
double dates,
husbands confused.

–Naomi Beth Wakan

Went long on ride
toward Providence.

–Bill Buck

I imagined

more than

office jobs.

—*Gretchen Vitamvas*

Overjoyed I'm not like
    my sister.

—*Elizabeth DeLamater*

Little German girl,
big American world.

—*Lisa Turner*

Hope my obituary spells
"debonair" correctly.

—*Gregg Easterbrook*

Just in:
boyfriend's gay.
Merry Christmas.

—*Seshie Hargett*

Traded mastheads for
Texas desert sky.

—*Whitney Joiner*

Lucky sperm club entrant
wins life.

—*Steve Conlin*

Was father, boys died,
still sad.

—*Ronald Zalewski*

Tried everything once,
few things twice.

—*Ed Zevetski*

Baptist Mom. Jewish Dad. Atheist.
Surprised?

—*Sara Faith Alterman*

**Cheated organizational
systems but never people.**

—*Ryan Bright*

Asked and
    answered,
    asshole,
    next question.

—*Joe Lockhart*

Really, doing fine,
thanks for asking.

—*Fuzzy Gerdes*

I'd rather be watching a movie.

—*Lawrence Levi*

Never could resist overachieving.

—*Chris Harris*

Her blue eyes
capture the distance.

—*Sonya Cheuse*

Born with glaucoma . . .
fading to black . . .

—*Susan Giusto*

I watched a lot of television.

—Adam Hirsch

Oh shit! No way? Yeah
dude.

—Ned Vizzini

Girls from the Bronx are
different.

—Arielle Basch

Five feet, but in
your face.

—Toby Berry

**Born bald. Grew hair.
Bald again.**

—A. J. Jacobs

Mistook streetlight for
the moon. Climbed.

—Zack Wentz

Boyfriend in bed,
still a lesbian?

—Cheryl Burke

I wrote a book about
this.

—Vittorio Giannini

Wanted to live forever,
died trying.

—Syona Luciferina

Hugged some trees,
then burned them.

—Tom Price

Happy child,
wild teenager,
adult anarchist.

—Dar Wolnik

Right place,
right time,
good lawyer.

—Ben Brown

**To paraphrase William
Faulkner: I endured.**

—Don Willmott

To make a long story short . . .

—Jace Albao

Famished, I had
seconds . . .
and thirds.

—Richard Strager

Lazy Renaissance man
settles for dilettantism.

—*Bradley Lyons*

Raised a palimpsest,
by many voices.

—Saba Cambone

Arab hillbilly goes to New
York.

—Alex Cummings

Full life; impossible to
summarize in

—Matt Love

Was rebellious teen.
Now raising one.

—Michelle Ganon

I have not done it all.

—Aaron Knoll

Woke up,

fell down,

    exited sideways.

—Jim Clupper

A new memoir every five years.

—Srini Rajagopalan

`My second grade teacher was right.`

—Janelle Brown

Rather sing than stay to chat.

—Keri Willson

Someone had to pay the bills.

—David Kuizenga

**Didn't fit in then;
still don't.**

-Bob Fingerman

I love my lady . . . and
bacon.

-Jeff Walton

**Buried gold long ago.
Can't find.**

-Maureen Barnes

Later-life serendipity
led to Authorland.

-Jeff Schult

A man, a plan, hot damn.

-L. Levyne

Revenge is living well,
without you.

—Joyce Carol Oates

I forgot I have memory loss.

–Mary Hynes

Underachieving . . . but willing to overcompensate halfheartedly.

–Frank J. Lepiane

A Brooklyn lawyer.
Sewer to Sue-er.

–Mo Mann

Outcast.

Picked last.

Surprised them all.

–Rachel Pine

Country girl seeks,
finds, abandons city.

–Jenny Rose Ryan

What did you say? I'm deaf.

—*Karen Putz*

Became my mother.
Please shoot me.

—*Cynthia Kaplan*

Kinetosis, hemihypertrophy, testicular elephantiasis; pleasureboat recalcitrant.

—*Roderick Maclean*

Explained Hitler, Shakespeare.
Couldn't explain self.

—*Ron Rosenbaum*

```
If there's more,
I want it.
```

—*Alex Hart*

It's like forever,
only much shorter.

—*Pete DeVito*

God, grant me patience.
Right now.

—*Michael Castleman*

Cancer for sure. Still no cure.

—*Jenn Siebel*

Relatively famous parents,
very low self-esteem.

—*Molly Jong-Fast*

Pitched. Pitched. Pitched. Wrote.
Revised. Revised.

—*Andrew Adam Newman*

Lazy programmer,
ugly runner,
NASCAR dad.

—*Frank Gilroy*

Woman with man's name—
thanks, parents!

—Curtis Sittenfeld

Born lucky, striving to die
worthy.

—Julia Carpenter

Tequila made her

clothes fall off.

—Susanne Broderick

After Manson,
my life became dull.

—Allan Sorensen

I told you I was crazy.

—Michaline Babich

Topless dancer. Circus clown. Spy. Writer.

—Susan DiRende

Sometimes it rains.
Sometimes I smile.

—Peter Hermann

I play dress-up for a living.

—Melissa Nicholl

Where the hell are
my keys?

—Brady Udall

Bank robber,
prison-humbled,
confesses all.

—Joe Loya

Found transvestite
hooker. Travis is pleased.

—Larry Tewksbury

She always wore socks to bed.

—Myfanwy Collins

Not as blond as I look.

—Ellen Meister

Often alone,
office drone,
feisty crone.

—Patty Quickert

`Horny small-town boy`

`becomes writer.`

—Kevin Sampsell

I closely resemble
my uncle Fred.

—Brian Van Nieuwenhoven

Well, I thought
it was funny.

—Stephen Colbert

Strived to become
    everything I didn't.

—*Richard Tomas*

Let's just be friends,
she said.

—*Mike Pfaffroth*

Happenstance, she thought—
but maybe not.

—*Amelia Allard*

Chemistry? No. Law?
No. Motherhood? Yes!

—*Anneliese Dickman*

I died at an early age.

—*John Coyne*

Lived like no tomorrow;
tomorrow came.

—*C. C. Keiser*

Date with geek yields
chip-filled life.

—*Robin Raskin*

**I couldn't possibly
fuck him again.**

—*Theodore Bouloukos*

Learned everything from
words, pictures, love.

—*Dan Goldman*

This imperfect life,
perfect for perfectionist.

—*Sarah Gardner*

Forgot to say I love her.

—*Omi Castanar*

Can't read all the time.
Bummer.

—*Rina Bander*

I wrote a poem.
Nobody cared.

—*Joe Heaps Nelson*

Put whole self in, shook about.

—*Melissa Delzio*

Not quite what I was
planning . . .

—*Summer Grimes*

From Colombia to Columbia: 27 years.

—Marisa Catalina Casey

Mojo search resumes,
impossible flowers bloom.

—*Nick Balaban*

I inhale battles.
I exhale victories.

—*William Heath*

Working with what God gave me.

—*David Schmoyer*

Former band nerd
dreams big dreams.

—*Jesse Poe*

Coffee. Coffee.
Water. Water.
Wine. Tea.

—*C. Hunter*

Southern queer teacher
plays, sings, laughs.

–Amanda Northrup

Same Mistakes.
Over and over again.

–Matthew Oransky

Still trying
to impress my dad.

–Shoshana Berger

Hatless, shirtless,
shitless. Still, I sang.

–Scott Hartwich

Girl loved Jesus.
Girl loves boys.

–Lindsay Robertson

We were our own
Springer episode.

—Michelle Hoogerwerf

. . . exalted philanderer of the
English language . . .

—Steven Ekstrom

**Laughter and inappropriate
humor since 1985.**

—Annie Jacobson

I am a cartwheel of mentorship.

—Anne Asher

Asked for love.
Received confusion.
Waiting.

—Irina Kendall

I always suffered
fools fairly well.

–*Richard Ford*

I re-met Lori after 27 years.

—*Alan Weinkrantz*

So devastated, no babies for me.

—*Jennifer Faulkner*

Nobel dad; tough act to follow!

—*Andreas Wettstein*

Me: fully reformed and
halfway happy.

—*Koren Zailckas*

```
Eat drink
man man
man man.
```

—*Michael Musto*

The day just kept getting better.

—Jeff Cranmer

Met lots of crazy famous people.

—Jonathan van Meter

Waited too long to get it.

—Rhona Yolkut

Took up photography. Got the shot.

—Keith MacDonald

Strange like cat. Smart like rat.

—Andrew Randall

I answer to the name Mom.

—*Lynne Chesterton*

Girls aren't 6'; I am 5'12.

—*Marlee Sayen*

Born in city that
doesn't exist.

—*Jackie Delamatre*

Disco jeans, 1977:
mine alone
finally.

—*Susie Park*

Fact checker by day,
liar by night.

—*Andy Young*

House of boarding passes,
like cards.

—*Mike Kuniavsky*

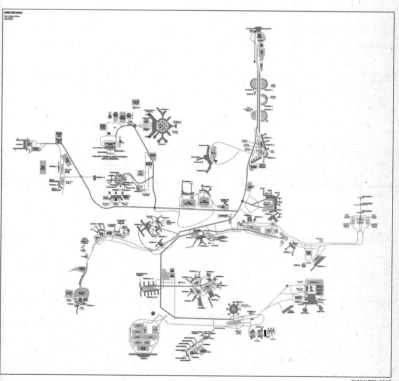

Weird quiet girl
fading from view.

—*Felicia Sullivan*

Four eyes are better than two.

—*Marissa Walsh*

Shot my penis in photo
booth.

—*Jeffrey Zeldman*

After which he was never sane.

—*Aleksandar Hemon*

**Gay Puerto Rican in
straight clothing.**

—*Ryan Roman*

Yes, singing rocks,
but money calls.

—Jonathan Cogswell

Almost nothing was
under my control.

—Joel Stein

Sold clocks carved out of
soap.

—Aaron Fagan

Learned. Forgot. Better
off relearning anyway.

—Brian DeLeeuw

More broken bones
than broken
hearts.

—Evan Rosler

Suburban girl tries
to make bad.

—*Sari Wilson*

Wife: one;
Degrees: two;
Arrests: seven.

—*Patrick J. Sauer*

Coulda, shoulda, woulda:
a regretful life.

—*Joe Maida*

These sails have never
settled long.

—*Justin Kownacki*

Let me in, you
narrative whore.

—*C. McClosky*

Fearlessness is the mother of reinvention.

—*Arianna Huffington*

It got better after middle age.

—Ruth Haworth

God who? Oh, him. No thanks.

—Carin Rhoden

Seeking route,
not sure of destination.

—Gary Belsky

Divorced! Thank God
for Internet personals.

—Maryrose Wood

Cheese is
the essence
of life.

—Mary Lynch

I waste time looking for love.

—*Sean Gannett*

Vietnam Protests.
Equality Protests.
Disability Protests.

—*Ron Kendricks*

My family did not
kill me.

—*David Sampliner*

Things happen because
I see holes.

—*Susan Chi*

Serial missed
connections
end with you.

—*Liz Brown-Inz*

Born in California.
Then nothing happened.

—*Mark Harris*

Named Hope. How else to be?
—Hope Hall

Straight jacket on
the gentle cycle.
—Stewart Rudy

Love Brooklyn,
but London still calls.
—Sarah Butterworth

Tickle, trample,
come back for more.
—Kathryn Waggener

I still secretly read
wedding magazines.
—Lestlie Berryhill

Asian, white trash Scranton.
Let's Polka.

—*Jeannie Lee*

Eat to live, live to eat.

—*Tim Toomey*

The freaks, they
always find me.

—*Ginger Lime*

Wildly crooked,
unlikely to be straightened.

—*lê thi diem thúy*

Got a pony, broke my arm.

—*Layne Bell*

Should have learned
to count.

-*David Wheatley*

dam smart—
never lerned to
spel.

-*Rachel Ehrlich*

My ancestors were
accented cow herders.

—Nina Moog

    Filled blank spaces with ambitious
    endeavors.

—Adam Schachner

```
Gin joints. Love affairs.
No relation.
```

—Dean Ellis

I traveled each
and every highway.

—Sebastian Buhai

Widowed. Forging reluctantly
forward with faith.

—TerriAnn Ferren

Still a very bad Mormon. Yay!

—Marsha Brown

This Tolstoy gets
no Oprah promotion.

—Victor Pelevin

Political stance makes
my family crazy.

—Steve Collins

Once was blind.
Now I see.

—David Hansen

Good things happen
to bad people.

—Michael Malice

162

Secret of life:

marry an Italian.

—*Nora Ephron*

Slightly flabby,
slightly fabulous,
trying hard.

—*Amy Friedman*

Palindromic novels fall
apart halfway through.

—*Chuck Clark*

Saw clearly after blind date. Marriage!

—*Saralee Rosenberg*

Thank god the suicide
attempt failed.

—*Rhett Miller*

Made labor-saving software: thousands
unemployed.

—*George Girton*

I hear nothing and see everyone.

—*Eunice Chang*

Secretly, I dream of
my ex-boyfriend.

—*Rosally Sapla*

Unfortunately,
there was no other way.

—*Atom Robinson*

A daydream, or so it seemed.

—*Eva Meszaros*

She danced, and
did little else.

—*Sarah Cost*

Came out.
Went in.
Came out.

—*Earl Adams*

Only black girl.
Fierce woman now.

—*Courtney Kemp Agboh*

My wife made me do it.

—*Jeffrey Yamaguchi*

Nature, nurture, lost, found, lost, found?

—*Sarah Saffian*

Other people's trash:
show and teller.

—*Jason Bitner*

birth
bris
bed
bath
and
beyond

—*Barry Blitt*

Like an angel. The fallen kind.

—*Rick Bragg*

Full of tequila and bad ideas.

—*Buck Johnston*

Lived in America.
Came back different.

—*Nigel French*

Lehmann-Haupt, yeah;
not that one.

—*Rachel Lehmann-Haupt*

Expected prime rib;
ended with hamburger.

—*Bernard Lam*

Drew on walls,
creative for life.

—*DeAnna Sandoval*

Unborn baby,
   dancing belly,
      arriving soon.

—*Tami Piccione*

Watchful crooked girl:
Comes with ink.

—*Erin Cressida Wilson*

Committed voluntarily,
until trying to leave.

—*Michael Holland*

When all else fails, start
running.

—*Dean Karnazes*

Carnivore and herbivore birth
magical omnivore.

—*Morgan Spurlock*

Never going to
have a dog.

—*Lily Redman*

Asked to quiet down; spoke
louder.

—*Wendy Lee*

My computer screen tells it all.

—*James Browne*

Indelibly tenacious,
I read and breed.

—*Shawna Lisk-Sprester*

Catholic girl. Jersey.
It's all true.

—*Mary Elizabeth Williams*

Don't marry a lawyer, be one.

—Deborah Schneider

Still waiting for you to ask.

—Alice Massey

Ex-addict now addicted
to book deals.

—Susan Shapiro

When talk matters,
make it count.

—Phil Liggett

Love New York;
Hate Self. (Equally.)

—David Rakoff

My penultimate act is to imbibe.

—Alex Twersky

Mmm, tea.

So stereotypical.

Rule Britannia!

—Paul O'Brien

Arty dad, rocker mom,
crazy childhood.

—Summer Pierre

Ordering soup for two, for one.

—Dan Silverman

Still here despite
logic and likelihood.

—Elisha Marshall

```
She read too much . . .
into everything.
```
—Jessica Reed

Father, son, both hit by cars.

—Gordon Hurd

Women's magazine
employee now
misogynist novelist.

—Stephanie Lessing

I didn't skateboard
nearly often enough.

—Kevin Wilkins

Internet famous,
for what that's worth.

—Ron Hogan

Sometimes at night I lay lonely.

–Mark Jaynes

**Deported once,
legal now—Green Card**.

–Michael Kaminer

I didn't walk off a roof.

–Tobin Levy

Say no now, I
now know.

–Steve Woodruff

Left house one day
for cigarettes.

–Sheila Ryan

What?
Lemony Snicket?
Lemony Snicket?
What?

—*Daniel Handler*

Made some good choices,
got lucky.

—*Matthew Kett*

```
Jew-born.
Yeshiva-educated.
Date goyim.
```

—*Abby Ellin*

Pop split; I write him in.

—*Sepideh Saremi*

True love was prevented
by leprosy.

—*Peter Hayward*

Pay attention to
me! Go away.

—*Kathy Rogers*

Big hair, big heart, big hurry.

—Larry Smith

Melancholy marvel at how
everything connects.

—Lawrence Weschler

Climbing, porn, crack,
science. Still bored.

—Lenny Oliker

I'm the fine print;
read closely.

—Kristina Grish

Ran east, ran west, ran late.

—Susie Smith

Will draw for
food and coffee.

—*Molly Crabapple*

Most Turkish Kurd, most
Kurdish Turk.

—Yasar Kemal

Tall, dark, handsome:
Single, content, uncommunicative.

—Mark Grace

Do as say, not as did.

—Emily Gordon

Good, evil use the same font.

—Arthur Harris

Detergent girl:
Bold. Tide. Cheer. All.

—Martha Clarkson

Never a bridesmaid;
always a bride.

—Anne Allisoni

I fell out of the
nest.

—Jason Logan

More than yesterday,
less than tomorrow.

—Nichiren Nahuel Palombo

I don't nibble. I bite.
Hard.

—Matthew Torres

Open road, no map.
Great Scenery.

—Tom Gabbay

Maybe you had to be
there.

—*Roy Blount Jr.*

Right brain working
left brain job.

—Dave Terry

Life behind a
microphone
gets lonely.

—Crystal Kash

Spent longing for
the seventh word.

—Ron Bel Bruno

Five continents down; two to go.

—Virginia Graham

Affection. Erection.
No protection.
Injection. Infection.

—Colleen Zachary

Speaks mind especially when losing it.

—*Ellis Reid*

He knew her bruises would fade.

—*Colin Stanton*

Indeterminate.
Not enough data for conclusion.

—*Ian Grant*

Tunneling underground, lured
deep by ghosts.

—*Danielle Trussoni*

I got herpes, in my pants.

—*Daniel Moyer*

Veni, vidi,
but haven't vici yet.

—*Meenakshi Nandini*

Hid for a while. Not anymore.

—Ginger Voight

I came, I saw, I concurred.

—Cris Anitsirhc

Afraid of mirrors,
too many marshmallows.

—Lihi Lasslo

Bought American Dream.
More like nightmare.

—Harry McCoy

I was concerned
about my obituary.

—James Dunn

Born red closet reborn SF queer.

—David Boyer

Youngest of four girls
turns fifty.

—Judi Kolenda

Saw the sky and
started walking.

—Mark Sundeen

Learned eventually,
Billy Crystal, not Salinger.

—Ben Kaplan

Once born,
now old,
soon gone.

—Andre Vandal

We were married in the snow.

—Polly and Andrew McLean

Photograph by Sean Graff

My life, in Mexico, is strange.

—Cosima Rose

Awkward girl takes chances.
Fun ensues.

—Charlotte Riley

The light that night was perfect.

—Lara Swimmer

Better living through chemistry,
sans love.

—Greg Rainwater

I auditioned.
I got the
part.

—Faith Hoffman

Entire story written
with quotidian nouns.

—Tim Batton

Losing your identity can be
fearsome.

—Robyn Crawford

Giraffe born to a farm family.

—Grant Langston

Lived life,
playing metal,
went deaf.

—M. Kincaid

I write stories. They come true.

—Rebecca Woolf

Struggling Southern eccentric
finding my happiness.

—Leigh Ann Apanites

Act two curtain brought
dramatic improvements.

—*John Godfrey*

Saw a glimpse,

should have risked.

—*Lori Flaherty*

Hey Red, order up! Chop! Chop!

—*Patty Griffin*

Somehow, she lived
without an iPod.

—*Jennifer Crouser*

Last words,
our daughter,
too soon.

—*Steve Allen*

Killed. Loved.
Got high on everything.

—*David Booth*

Lonely, frothy kisses,
then only spite.

—*Stephania Serena*

Dead mom watching. I'll be good.

—*Israel Hyman*

Became more like myself
every year.

—*Eddie Sulimirski*

Rich in degrees
and student loans.

—*Barb Piper*

He was happy being a flasher.

—Fred Telegdy

Old and married.
Hot classmates. Sigh.

—Bill Johnson

Nerdy, wordy,
learned to shut up.

—Caren Lissner

```
Type A personality.
Type B capability.
```

—Keith Lang

High school dropout
but college graduate.

—Mary Beth Nalin

Dreamed of endless love.
Awoke alone.

—Mohammad Fatayerji

Adolescence, internet,
internet, internet, internet,
death.

—Josh Rosenfield

We were each other's
favorite person.

—Montana diLemonada

```
Surname rhymes with
   profanity.
   Childhood torture.
```

—Noah Smit

Must remember: people,
gadgets. That order.

—Brian Lam

Learned to live with great loss.

—Michele Wytko

Sex overrated.
Went and got castrated.

—Alex Warren

Occassionally wrong but
never in doubt.

—Layne Butler

Illiterate poet saw
far too much.

—Robert Strassburg

WASP wants
to be soul
man.

—Scott Pratt

Me see world!
Me write stories!

—*Elizabeth Gilbert*

Alabama boy said hallalujah,
wrote memoirs.

—*Paul Thornton*

Normal female blogs
for a living.

—*Sarah Weinman*

Accidents cause people—
son is wonderful.

—*Laurie Reinhart*

Impoverished black male.
Harvard Law bound.

—*Robert Young*

Leaving:
I toss blame like grenades.

—*Tanya Jarrett*

Born ready, bad eyes and all.

—Hua Hsu

Thought long and hard.
Got migraine.

—Lisa Levy

Ten strikes against me,
hit homerun.

—Maxine Jennings

Despite disorders, jafroed
jewboy gets girl.

—Michael Eisner

Older orphan,
creates family with friends.

—Theresa Neinas

That Kiss song says it all.

—*James Hampton*

I can resist everything
except temptation.

—*Carolina Conte*

Should have risked

asking, he sighed.

—*Gino Serdena*

Here: Macaca! There: American!
Where, beloved?

—*Mitali Perkins*

Never should've done that first line.

—*Joshua MacPhetridge*

Adopted?
Are you fucking
shitting me?

—*Darius Logan*

Traveling the road,
    writing science fiction.

—Henry Melton

Hard to write poems
from prison.

—Ellen Goldstein

Born in abject obscurity;
never escaped.

—James Blum

Friends all Jewish.
I'm merely neurotic.

—Brian Mahon

Suburban Christian child.
Hippie agnostic adult.

—Shannon Barnes

Writing and drawing
brought me here.

—*Gabrielle Bell*

Alaskan hippie kid. Escaped via Ph.D.

—Melanie Brewer

Clumsy girl found adventure.
Also, bruises.

—Rebecca Campbell

Jury believed me; prison awaits him.

—Jessica Yu

Realized childhood dream
doesn't pay bills.

—Nicole Williams

Mostly waited for the big stuff.

—Jennifer Smith

Taught lies.
 Discovered truth.
  Neither matters.

—Gautham Nagesh

Born into a life
worth living.

—Cher Tushiah

Met Jesus early, then ran fast.

—Jessica Thompson

I'm not afraid of
anything anymore.

—Kathryn Hammond

The road diverged; I took it.

—Rachel Farris

Eight thousand orgasms.

Only one baby.

—*Neal Pollack*

Loved a man, then a woman.

—Kate Evans

Product of obscure
American colonial
ancestors.

—Randy Seaver

Brainy widowed sexpot
raises hell, kids.

—Jennifer Johnson

Wounded girl turns life into
stories.

—Farai Chideya

The militant who became a monk.

—Mike Adams

Born in Baghdad,
I said enough.

—Shwan Taha

Most successful accomplishments
based on spite.

—Scott Birch

Haunting dad,
spotlight mom,
retrieving marriage.

—Nell Casey

She left Texas none too soon.

—Jen Worrell

Carries flask for
unsociable social events.

—Janina Williams

He wore dresses.
This caused messes.

—Josh Kilmer-Purcell

Man, slightly disgruntled,
may throw poo.

—Egan Fowler

It's all about me,
isn't it?

—Daniel Halpern

My memoir? You can't be serious.

—Dan Menaker

EDITOR. Get it?

—Kate Hamill

I always took the
joke too far.

—Thomas Hamill

Big nose, British chicken legs:
beautiful!

—Jen Gabel

I will never be
quite finished.

—J. P. Hoban

Learning disability, MIT.
Never give up.

—Joe Keselman

Glory developing vital loving
fighting life.

—Josh Lucas

Just a rockin' readin'
knittin' kitten.

—Emmeline Friedman

Looking to know everything
   about everything.

> —*Tor Andersen*

Philosophical teen,
   surrounded but sometimes lonely.

> —*Nehemiah Blazek*

Retired music teacher
enjoys life's symphonies.

> —*Caroline Baker*

Liked by all. Known by
   few.

> —*Zell Williams*

Age eleven:
became a middle
child.

> —*Matt Farrell*

Dad wore leather pants in Reno.

—John Falk

Illustration by Bob Salpeter

Worse fates have befallen better men.

—*Stanley Morgenstern*

18 years old,
first kiss uncertainty.

—*Jerrica Moore*

Polio gave me my happy life.

—*Ruth Thompson*

Big heart protected
by sharp tongue.

—*Kris Kleindienst*

I tried. It was not
enough.

—*Robert McCarty*

Learned to say no too late.

—*Jonathan Engle*

There will be no
beautiful corpse.

—*Sharon Lewis*

You must be fifty to
understand.

—*Rev. Henri Breitenkam*

Loved God, reason,
  simplicity; authored
  books.

—*Patricia Williams*

He always liked to live
fast.

—*Jesse Burkett*

Former child star
    seeks love, employment.

—*Justin D. Taylor*

Didn't pull out.
Downhill from there.

—*Roger Daubach*

Fears commitment, debt.
Attracts spouse, house.

—*Beth Grundvig*

Rubber nipples,
    dimpled thumbs,
    Camel Lights.

—*Dawn Ryan*

Smart, humble, shy.
Notice me, please?

—*Ryan Kucera*

Wasn't born a redhead;
fixed that.

—Andie Grace

Found a demon to love forever.

—Aaron Olson

Made costly mistakes,
learned valuable lessons.

—Ricky Roach

Green eyes,
freckled skin,
waiting womb.

—Heather Thompson

Naively expected logical world.
Acted foolish.

—Emily Thieler

Tell your story.
That's my story.

—*Andy Goodman*

These words are
yours to keep.

—*Alec Ounsworth*

On the seventh
word, he rested.

—*Stephen J. Dubner*

Index